THROUGH HIS EYES

CLAIRE ELIZABETH GROSE

Copyright © 2020 by Claire Elizabeth Grose

Compiled and edited by Michael Grose and June Kennedy

All rights reserved. No portion of this publication may be reproduced, stored in a retrieval system or transmitted in any form by any means – electronic, mechanical, photocopying, recording, or any other –except for brief quotation in printed reviews, without the prior written permission of the publisher.

Unless indicated otherwise, all scripture quotations in this book are from the following source:

The Good News Bible: The Bible in Today's English Version (TEV) © 1976 by the American Bible Society. Used with permission.

ISBN 978-0-6486884-2-6

Author contact information - clairegrose.heartmatters@gmail.com

Version 1.0

DEDICATION

This book is dedicated to Andrew and Bianca
Precious gifts from my Lord

CONTENTS

DEDICATION IV

CONTENTS V

PREFACE VIII

ACKNOWLEDGEMENTS X

    PART ONE 1

        MY DAILY PRAYER 4
        THROUGH HIS EYES 5
        HEART OF HEARTS 6
        HIS HALLOWED FACE 7
        I FELT YOUR LOVE TODAY 8
        EACH ONE OF US UNIQUE 9
        SEEK HIM 10
        CALLING THE DAWN 11
        DRIFT WITH CHRIST 14
        EYES OF ETERNITY 15
        A RUSH OF PURE LOVE 16
        THE SHORTEST PRAYERS 17
        MIGHTY ANCHOR 18
        RAINBOW JOY 19
        A MOUNTAIN OF LOVE 20
        MOTHER EARTH RESTS 21
        EXQUISITE BEAUTY 22
        ANOTHER YEAR HAS PASSED 23
        ETERNAL IS HIS WORD 26
        CUSTOM MADE 27
        YOUR BEAUTY 28
        SISTERS AND BROTHERS 29

    PART TWO 30

        TIME IS IN HIS HANDS 33
        QUIETEN THOUGHTS OF DAY 34
        QUEST FOR LIFE 35
        SHOW YOUR LOVE 36

IN YOUR EYES	37
RAYS OF LOVE	38
DINNER FOR TWO	41
OPEN HOUSE	43
SOUL TIME	44
EVERY DAY IS A NEW PAGE	45
QUIET MOMENTS	46
EYES OF LOVE	47
TRUST IN YOUR FAITH	50
STRENGTH WITHIN	51
HIS STOREHOUSE	52
WHAT'S NEXT	53
INNER STRENGTH	54
OPEN MY HEART	55
ANGELS ON EARTH	58
TRUST THROUGH AND THROUGH	59
HARBOUR OF PEACE	60
CHANGE YOU TO THE CORE	61
SHEPHERD OF ALL	62
A PURPOSE FOR TODAY	63
WHEN WORDS ARE LOST IN FATHOMS DEEP	64
YOUR HOLY PLAN	65
KEEP ME COVERED	66
EMOTION	67
CLAIM HIS RIGHTEOUSNESS	68
WINTER CHILLS	69
PART THREE	70
SONS AND DAUGHTERS OF THE KING	73
HE CAN'T WAIT TO MEET YOU	74
HIS BELOVED	75
SEA OF WORDS	76
WE ALL NEED THE SAVIOUR'S LOVE	77
SERVE OF LOVE	78
MARCH IN STEP	81
REACH FOR THE SAVIOUR	82

PEACE TIME	83
QUESTIONS AND ANSWERS	84
NEVER GIVE UP ON HOPE	85
MY FAINTING HEART	86
PART FOUR	87
AS IT IS WRITTEN	90
A BRAND NEW LOVE	91
THE COMMUNION CUP	92
HE LIVES TODAY	95
THE WONDER OF HIS LOVE	96
CHRISTMAS EVE SUPPERS	99
FRANKINCENSE, MYRRH AND GOLD	100
JOY ON CHRISTMAS MORNING	101
I KNEW HIM FROM A CHILD	102

PREFACE

Two things I just wanted to say about this book are, why I started writing and how I came by the title.

I grew up in the 1950's-1960's in Adelaide, South Australia, my life was pretty simple but wonderful. I was very lucky to have a secure family life, and my Mum and Dad brought the family up to treat others with respect, do the right thing, be courteous, and respect your elders. We had a strict upbringing and even as adults our parents never criticized us but encouraged us to do our best in life. They were "Aussie battlers" but we always managed to make it through the tough times!

They were people of integrity and cared about others and instilled that into our family.

Church was a big part of our lives growing up. We went to Sunday School at an early age and progressed up through the appropriate groups as we got older.

Youth groups, camps and church anniversaries were all important to the whole family. We competed in church sports teams, basketball and tennis with other parishes across Adelaide. Life-long friendships were in the making and cherished golden memories to look back on that would never fade.

Bible stories, hymns and choruses were all part of getting to know Jesus. This nurturing finally led me to the day Jesus came knocking on my heart's door. Being filled with the Holy Spirit is something I will never forget and the overwhelming power of His love that filled my whole being and propelled me to the front of the hall to give my heart to Him. No words can fully describe the joy I felt. That was in February 1968, I was 14 years of age. He has been my Shining Light ever since, and lives within me always.

So I thank my beautiful Mum and Dad for the way they raised me and for the foundation of knowing Jesus' love.

It was in His love that I started to write, in the autumn of 1993. My journey has brought me to this book "Through His Eyes". The title came to me when I was thinking of how God looks at the world and what His expectations are of us and how He longs for us to love one another, be kind, compassionate, help someone.

"This, then, is what I command you: love one another." (John 15:17)

When preparing this book, I wanted to focus on the Book of John in the Gospels because I felt it was the most loving book which writes of Jesus teaching His disciples that the most important thing in life is to love. "Do not be worried and upset, Jesus told them". "Believe in God and believe also in me." (John 14:1)

When I was a young Christian this scripture really spoke to me and became the foundation that I built my faith on. It gave me strength and courage as I began life in the workforce at the age of 16. Coming from a sheltered upbringing it was my life-line to self-confidence and adapting to social life at work.

The poems reflect the everyday feelings and emotions that we feel as we meet the challenges of life and how the great magnitude of God's love can help us rise above them.

I pray you will seek His eternal counsel in your everyday life and receive His grace and mercy in "Through His Eyes".

Many of these writings have been my first words of whispered prayer, so much that I have been moved to write them down at once and continue on in His wonderful and absolute love.

Together we write as He provides my inspiration.

All glory to Him, my precious Lord Jesus!

ACKNOWLEDGEMENTS

My heartfelt thanks to my beloved family, my Mum and Dad, Lilly and Kenny, and my siblings Jeanette, June, Carol, Gloria and Lynne, for their never ending encouragement and support to me. To the rest of the family, you are all a precious link that joins us together.

To Michael and Andrew for your continual support to me in fulfilling my passion of writing poems for the Lord to help others through His Word.

A huge thank you to Junie for editing my poems and the coffees and lunches we enjoyed along the way.

To Joy Furnell for her Crown of Thorns drawing, you have an amazing gift, thank you. To my friends and Church families, thank you for your love and support.

Special thanks to Salisbury Uniting Church, Adelaide for the Cross photo.   Used by permission.

Many thanks to June and Hugh, Carol and Den, Lindsay, Christopher and Justine, Karen and Jeff, Jane and Scott for photographs.

To my beautiful sons, Michael and Andrew, thank you for loving me, and I am so glad He gave you to me. I will love you forever. To your partners Andrea and Bianca and also my grandchildren, I love you all so much.

To you the reader, thank you for picking this book up and I pray you will find His peace and love on the pages ahead.

May He shower you all with His love and blessings.

PART ONE

"…My Father will love whoever loves me; I too will love him and reveal myself to him."

John 14 : 21

THROUGH HIS EYES

HIS LOVE OVERFLOWS…

"…Whoever believes in me, streams of life-giving water will pour out from his heart."

John 7 : 38

MY DAILY PRAYER

Be with me, stay with me,
Close by my side,
Fill me with your peace and love,
So my spirit shall surely fly
To the heights in your love,
As only you can give,
Prepare me for this day ahead,
So in me you'll always live.

THROUGH HIS EYES

When you think of God's love,
What comes to mind?
How He cares for each of us,
Try looking through His eyes.

His love is eternal,
It never fades away,
It's always full measure,
It's with us every day.

Even though we let Him down,
The way we act and think,
But as we are His children,
To Him we are surely linked.

To care for each other
As He commanded us to,
To live by the heart,
That's what His love will do.

His love will change us,
To His mark we will rise,
His love will rule your heart,
When you look through His eyes.

HEART OF HEARTS

Inside your heart of hearts
Your deepest feelings lie,
Only you know
The cares that abide inside.

But you can give them all
To the King of Kings today,
He will gather them in His hands
And take them all away.

He knows your heart of hearts,
Every detail hidden deep,
He can wash those cares away
If Him you truly seek.

So give your heart of hearts,
Share your joy or tears,
He wants all of you
Because to Him you are so dear.

HIS HALLOWED FACE

When I see His hallowed face,
Pure love is all I know,
Sunbeams radiate around,
Blessings from Him flow.

When I see His hallowed face,
He brings His love divine,
My cares and woes just slip away,
His joy I surely find..

When I see His hallowed face,
Peace comes to me,
He is God's beloved Son,
I bow on bended knee.

When I see His hallowed face,
Glory from Him shines,
He rules over creation,
I'm so glad He is mine.

I FELT YOUR LOVE TODAY

Thank you Lord for your love
That touches my heart so,
It makes me feel so close to you
To feel your Spirit flow.

Peace and calm come to me
In a gentle flowing stream,
Like ripples on the surface
That make their way to me.

My heart and soul are shining
As you pour your love within,
This peace I want forever,
I'm so glad you live within.

EACH ONE OF US UNIQUE

His gifts to us are so unique,
Each one special in His eyes,
He made us all differently
That we can't deny.

Every heart beats to a tune,
On a different path,
Many different walks of life,
Many people going past.

He created us in His image,
Though without sin we'll never be,
What a privilege to behold,
To be made like Thee.

There's not one life on this earth,
Just like any other,
Our earthly form so different
Many people to discover.

The precious gifts bestowed within,
By His holy hand,
When we know His pure love,
We will understand.

SEEK HIM

Take your heart to a quiet place,
Hush the thoughts of day,
Align yourself with the King of Kings
Who takes your sin away.

There you'll find His pure love
And know His ecstasy,
Calm and peace will own your soul
You'll be forever free.

Seek Him and come into His fold,
He will welcome you with open arms,
His divine love will touch your soul,
He'll anoint you with His balm.

Seek the Lord of Heaven
And invite Him into your heart,
Open the door to Eternal Life
You will stroll His heavenly path.

CALLING THE DAWN

Triumphant song arises
In chords sweet and proud,
Calling the Dawn is heard,
Birds awake from night time shroud.

The veil of night drifts away
As crimson clouds appear,
Calling the Dawn parades,
Are heard from far and near.

Tunes for the Master,
Like honey is soothing balm,
Heralds the day ahead
Into His loving arms.

Calling the Dawn makes Jesus smile
As His babes entertain,
Bring pure joy to His heart,
An "intro" for every day.

THROUGH HIS EYES

LOOK TO JESUS…

"…I have come in order that you might have life – life in all its fullness."

John 10 : 10

DRIFT WITH CHRIST

Close your eyes drift with Christ,
He holds you so dear,
He loves you more than you'll ever know,
He'll bear your hurts and fears.

Close your eyes drift with Him,
See Him on His Throne,
Claim His bounty of pure love,
Claim Him for your own.

Close your eyes drift with Him,
He is love divine,
He'll breathe on you eternal life
To live in countless time.

EYES OF ETERNITY

Open the door to Heaven,
Accept His love and grace,
You will have a friend forever
When you look upon His face.

You will find pure love
In the eyes that saw the first day,
Of His beautiful creation,
That takes your breath away.

You'll find a heart so big
That can love the world below,
He longs for your affection
So your faith can surely grow.

You'll find a smile divine
In His face of Light,
He is the King of Heaven,
You are precious in His sight.

So live for Eternity,
Prepared by God's Son,
Keep your eyes on the Master,
To truly feel His love.

A RUSH OF PURE LOVE

Reach out to His presence
Say what's on your mind,
You'll be so glad
That you gave Him the time.

He is always with you,
Speak to Him like you would a friend,
He loves you forever,
His faithfulness never ends.

Recognize His closeness
And His peace that He brings,
In early morning melodies
Or beautiful blooms in Spring.

A rush of pure love
That flows over your heart,
His Spirit comes to love you
And will never depart.

THE SHORTEST PRAYERS

Take the time
To whisper a prayer,
Just a few words
And He is there.

Right beside you
For you to carry on,
He'll never leave you
For you He longs.

To hear your words
However brief,
He wants to share your thoughts
From His mercy seat.

The shortest prayers
Still count to Him,
However soft
Are heard by the King.

MIGHTY ANCHOR

Belief in the King of Kings,
Is the strongest anchor you can ever own,
You will be saved forever
With Him who sits on His Throne.

He is the King of dreams,
He's planned them all for you,
Your life has been mapped out,
Each sunrise is brand new.

Whatever the day holds,
Be assured He's by your side,
Take hold of this mighty anchor,
He will be your guide.

Hold firm to this anchor,
Never let it go,
Please know, please know
He truly loves you so.

RAINBOW JOY

This gift that appears
When showers fall,
Brings His love
And lifts my all.

His colours so divine,
Truly thrill my soul,
Her curve is so perfect
A wonder from days of old.

Rainbow so awesome
Brings heavenly peace,
Brightens my day indeed,
Her joy will never cease.

A MOUNTAIN OF LOVE

Look to the Saviour
And what do you see?
A mountain of love
For you and me.

All things perfect
When we look to Him,
He will change us in His image
If in His love we live.

As little children
He wants us to come,
With a child-like faith,
For a mountain of love.

His mountain of love
Never gives up,
No matter what you've done,
To you He will come.

Yes a mountain of love
From that Holy Night,
If we would just believe,
He can make things right.

MOTHER EARTH RESTS

Morning fog blinds mountain tops,
Icy peaks and snowy lofts,
Purple mounds that rise and fall,
Dewy drapes dress plains and moors.

Biting wind that smacks the face,
Brittle leaves that rise to chase,
Dancing high in serenade,
Floating on icy waterways.

Mother Earth sleeps in winter chill,
The Master gives her rest until
Spring time buds burst forth on show,
Now sunshine gives the call for growth.

EXQUISITE BEAUTY

Breathe in His fragrance anytime
From sweet buds on the vine,
Perfumes flow pure within,
To thrill this heart of mine.

From stunning Rose and Daffodil,
Stylish Orchid and Jonquils,
Darling Marigold and Dahlia,
Regal Gerbera and Magnolia.

Pretty as Bluebell and Carnation,
Elegant Lily and Hydrangea,
Striking Tulip and Wisteria
Pretty as a picture!

Petite Daisy and Begonia,
Heartfelt Geranium and Poppy
Colourful Fuchsia and Petunia,
Sweet Chrysanthemum and Pansy.

Christmas Snowball and Agapanthus,
Forever Jacaranda and Jasmine,
Pretty Violet and Cyclamen,
Glorious Ranunculus and Lotus.

He created exquisite beauty
From His precious hand,
Thank you Lord for these blooms
That blossom on your command.

ANOTHER YEAR HAS PASSED

Another year has passed,
Time keeps marching on,
Precious Lord direct my path,
You know where I belong..

The months behind me
Are like a kaleidoscope,
Ups and downs, through thick and thin
You helped me to cope.

You want me to look ahead
To embrace another year,
I only have today
To work through, that is clear.

Each day I have you Lord
To share my plans ahead,
You will always be near,
To give me daily rest.

FOLLOW HIS PROMPTS…

"…I am the way, the truth, and the life;
No one goes to the Father except by me,…"

John 14 : 6

ETERNAL IS HIS WORD

Read His Word for inner strength
It will soothe the weary mind,
Rest for a while with His Word
Solace you will find.

His Word is still so powerful
As it was in ancient times,
His hand is still a shield
That protects this life of mine.

His words of love for all the world
More than the grains of sand,
Heal like a soothing balm,
He will take you by the hand.

He will comfort and embrace you
Through the pages of His Word,
Search and you will find His love,
Eternal is His Word.

CUSTOM MADE

I make plans for the future
Which I think are right for me,
But the Saviour owns the "blue print"
That He custom made for me.

He puts in place His helpers
With signs to direct my path,
But sometimes I don't see them
And keep going right on past.

Then I come to a crossroad
I wonder which way now,
So I go the way I think
And say "why am I here now?"

I used to go my merry way
And most times get totally lost,
But now I trust the Saviour
Who fully paid Calvary's cost.

YOUR BEAUTY

The sunsets carry your beauty Lord
That takes my breath away,
They speak your love in volumes,
The gift you give each day.

Your colours made in Heaven
By your pierced hands,
Pours out to the world,
Your glory makes a stand.

That's how you bring your love
In such a gentle way,
Lighting up the sky,
Your beauty will never fade.

So thank you Lord for sunsets
And the peace it brings to me,
You crown the end of day
In calm tranquility.

SISTERS AND BROTHERS

My sisters and brother share a bond
Which we've had from the start,
Whether we live close by
Or a world apart.

There's something so special
From the seed we bear,
Our bloodlines run together
And precious memories we all share.

The Saviour has His reasons
For distributing hearts around,
To fulfill His heavenly plan,
That's where we are bound.

Just like a beautiful garden
That flourishes in the Spring,
Our seeds will blend together,
What joy and love they bring.

So thank you beautiful parents
Who bought us into the world,
And your guiding hand to raise us,
We all have a story to tell.

PART TWO

"I am the bread of life,"
Jesus told them…

John 6 : 35

LISTEN …
FOR HIS WHISPERS…

"My sheep listen to my voice; I know them, and they follow me."

John 10 : 27

TIME IS IN HIS HANDS

Through His eyes of love
He waits patiently,
No matter how long it takes,
Time He doesn't need.

He longs for each of us
To claim Him as their own,
So He can live within
And make your heart His home.

A minute or an hour,
A decade or a thousand years,
Time He doesn't keep,
He will wipe away your tears.

His timing is perfect
According to His plan,
For answers to your prayers,
Time is in His hands.

He has His reasons
For each of us a plan,
Just be patient all is well,
Time is in His hands.

QUIETEN THOUGHTS OF DAY

Your clouds speak to me
And take my heart away
To a place of peace
Anytime on any day.

Shimmers of pink and musk
Threads of gold at dusk,
Melancholy time of day
Takes my heart away.

Your heavenly gift to give me joy
Every single day,
Clouds dusted with orange and mauve
Takes my heart away.

Crimson clouds come my way
To quieten thoughts of day,
I lift my eyes to the sky
Which takes my heart away.

QUEST FOR LIFE

As we search
Down the pathway of life,
Stay close to us Lord
Every day and every night.

Help us Lord
To make decisions in life,
In the quest of time
To turn from wrong to right.

We learn by our mistakes
And endure the cost,
We should count our gain
And not our loss.

My prayer for the world Lord
Is to search for peace,
Let there be strength in truth
To reign and never cease.

So in our quest for life
Whether it be big or small,
Guide our daily footsteps
To help us all stand tall.

SHOW YOUR LOVE

Show your love for the Saviour
Who knocks at your heart's door,
He comes with pure love
To save you ever more.

Show your love for the Saviour
When His Spirit touches you,
Your hearts will shine like pure gold,
You will feel brand new.

Show your love for the Saviour,
Help others with daily needs,
Show His love in your actions,
He will reward you indeed.

Show your love for the Saviour,
Praise Him in His Holy place,
Raise your arm in praise,
Accept His love and grace.

IN YOUR EYES

In your eyes my soul I see
That you gave to me,
Heaven's holy plan was born,
All the days I would meet.

In your eyes my heart I see
Your secret home within,
Filled with your Holy Spirit,
That's where your love begins.

In your eyes my all you see
This life you gave to me,
Whether I am weak or strong
I still belong to Thee.

RAYS OF LOVE

His rays of love point to the earth
Every morning and every night,
They reach north, south, east and west,
To the depths and to the heights.

His rays of love touch everyone
Who receives Him as their Lord,
Invite Him into your life,
And your heart will applaud.

His rays of love will change you
And wash you clean inside,
No words can explain the joy
When by His love you are baptized.

His rays of love will shroud you
Both day and night,
Your heart will know pure love
All the days of your life.

PONDER…
GOD IN HIS HEAVEN…

"There are many rooms in my Father's house, and I am going to prepare a place for you…"

John 14 : 2

DINNER FOR TWO

I long to see you standing
Before my eyes tonight,
Then dear, dear Lord
Everything would be alright.

To serve you at my table
The best of the best,
So we could eat together
And the food you would bless.

The finest wine I could find,
Is there any fit for the King?
To pass your lips of wonder
That spoke to stop the wind!

And conversation, what would we say?
To pass the time while we eat,
I think the contents of my heart
I would lay at your feet.

And the candle light would shine
In your eyes full of love
As they held my gaze completely,
You are the Son of God.

I never want to leave you,
So in my heart you'll always stay
Until the time you call me
Home, on my last day.

But through faith I see you now
And feel your love divine,
That's how it is for the present
While I wait until my time.

OPEN HOUSE

His Kingdom is an open house
For all who have heard His call,
He longs for our devotion
To give Him our all.

His open house is made of love,
The purest to be found,
It will last forever
Where there are no bounds.

He asks for simple faith,
To come as a little child,
Believe with an open heart
To make each day worthwhile.

Yes, He's prepared an open house
For all His beloved to come,
To live in His presence forever more
So we can live as one.

SOUL TIME

Soul time is quiet time,
I feel your presence near,
My focus is on you,
I bring my cares and fears.

I find your peace and calm
Deep within my soul,
Heavenly bliss I feel inside
Because you have made me whole.

So thank you Lord for soul time
When I focus on you above,
To cease my thoughts just for a while,
I come to you for love.

EVERY DAY IS A NEW PAGE

Every day is a new page
When golden skies awake,
Light filters through my room
As I pray for the new day.

For whatever comes my way,
I have to keep an open mind,
Every day is a new page,
God will be my guide.

So take Him on your journey
Whether it be long or short,
Ask for His strength and knowledge
To power your every thought.

Pray for His loving hand
To steady you on your way,
You only have to ask Him,
Every day is a new page.

QUIET MOMENTS

Take a quiet moment
Just for yourself,
Say a prayer to the Lord,
For His holy help.

He will hold your gaze
As you merge as one,
Lost in His love,
God's precious Son.

This quiet moment
You won't want to leave,
Feeling His joy
You truly will believe.

So just meet Him quietly,
Find time for Him,
Just whisper that prayer
You'll be so glad you did.

EYES OF LOVE

Eyes of love so tender
Full of love divine,
The Saviour shines His light
Through this heart of mine.

To make my eyes smile
With His pure love,
It comes within
From His heights above.

His goodness travels deep
To my soul alone,
Fills it with His Grace
Where He has made His home.

I give my heart completely
To you Lord of Lords,
With my eyes of love
It's you I adore.

ASK...
IN TRUST RECEIVE...

"...ask and you will receive, so that your happiness may be complete."

John 16 : 24

TRUST IN YOUR FAITH

Faith must carry you
When times are tough,
Emotion strikes a chord,
You want to say "enough"!

If you believe in the King of Kings
Your faith will carry you through,
Trust in Him completely,
You know He wants you to.

Ask Him daily
For His guidance and loving care,
You know He's right beside you,
He knows the why, how and where.

So, trust in your faith,
He will close and open doors,
All your days to come,
Forever He is yours.

STRENGTH WITHIN

When storm clouds hover overhead
And the heart feels shaky from words that were said,
And confidence just melts away,
The mind seems to lose its way.

Look to the Master for strength within,
He's always beside you, just call for Him,
Though problems overwhelm the mind,
Talk to the Master, courage you'll find.

Ask Him for strength within,
His calm He will always bring,
That moment when you seek His help,
His presence will be felt.

HIS STOREHOUSE

Forget any bad dreams from the past,
Welcome hope for today,
Take from His storehouse
Wisdom and strength will come your way.

Thank Him for His storehouse of wealth
For all His believers to help themselves,
Pray for whatever you need,
He will provide just wait and see.

His storehouse supplies never run out,
This you can never doubt,
Just welcome Him into your heart,
"Thank you" you will want to shout.

WHAT'S NEXT

What shall I be
And where do I go?
My course ahead
You planned long ago.

I have to do my best
With this life of mine,
To carry through each day
What's next shall I find.

So I ask for your shield
To protect me as I go,
Always be with me Lord,
What's next, only you know.

I pray for peace and truth
To lead me through life,
Whatever next comes along,
Give me your strength divine.

INNER STRENGTH

Read His word for inner strength
It will never let you down,
He's the only one who can soothe your heart,
His saving Grace is found.

Talk to the Saviour for inner strength,
He's waiting to take your hand
And shield you from the wounds within,
He always understands.

His everlasting arms
Are waiting to hold you close,
His inner strength will build you up
When you need it the most.

Call on His inner strength
To rise above your fears,
Ask for His love and power,
Your whispers He always hears.

OPEN MY HEART

If I open my heart to you Lord,
I will feel you near,
To forget the cares of the world
And know you'll take my fears.

If I open my heart to you Lord,
Your Spirit will live within,
You'll soothe my racing thoughts,
Peace and calm you will bring.

If I open my heart to you Lord,
For love and help along the way,
Reassurance will be mine,
By my side you'll always stay.

CALL ON HIM FOR PEACE...

"Do not be worried and upset," Jesus told them. "Believe in God and believe also in me."

John 14 : 1

ANGELS ON EARTH

There are angels on Earth Lord
To do your chosen work,
To help with a special need
Because you were the first.

The first to show us how to love,
To give a helping hand,
That's why there are angels on Earth
Who make your Holy stand.

There are angels on Earth
Who go the extra mile,
To bridge the gap of hopelessness,
To meet a need worthwhile.

There are angels on Earth
Who display your heavenly love,
Your very faithful servants
Bring hope from you above.

So thank you Lord, for your angels on Earth
Who love so endlessly,
You charge them with your power,
To bring us close to Thee.

TRUST THROUGH AND THROUGH

Take me to your realm above,
To forget my daily cares,
Help me put away my woes
To see your face so fair.

Your realm above is there for all,
Your home for us indeed,
We only have to believe in you
To receive a life so free.

You want us all to receive your love,
To walk daily with you
And know eternal joy is ours
If we trust you through and through.

No matter what comes our way
You are there that's true,
Waiting for our acknowledgement
To trust you through and through.

HARBOUR OF PEACE

When life deals a blow
That you just can't comprehend,
Your peace and calm is shattered
Time and time again.

There's a harbour of peace for you
Waiting patiently,
The Saviour Himself
Wants to soothe those choppy seas.

Take your fears to the harbour of peace,
He's waiting with precious balm,
To anoint your wounds so lovingly,
So your fears will turn to calm.

So drift in His harbour of peace
When life deals a blow,
Anchor yourself by His side,
His blessings you will know.

CHANGE YOU TO THE CORE

Mortal lives so complex,
Emotions running wild,
We must make time to stop
And think for a while.

Take time out for you
To recharge and heal yourself,
We all need peace and calm
So ask for the Saviour's help.

We know the highs and lows
That come along each day,
He can change you to the core
If you truly pray.

He will abide with you,
You will live forever more
In His glory and His splendor
That will change you to the core.

SHEPHERD OF ALL

Lord, you are the Great Shepherd
Who calls His sheep by name,
You always come to find them
When they fall or sometimes stray.

Sometimes in life we wander off
To explore on our own,
But you come to find us
And guide us back home.

We weather storms and sunshine
In the paddocks of life,
We look for comforting shelter
When things don't go right.

So look to the Shepherd of all,
Who loves His sheep unconditionally,
Wherever we are in the world,
In His care we always will be.

A PURPOSE FOR TODAY

Lord, help me
To have a purpose for today,
To shake off the blues
And to find my way.

To be positive
For the next twenty four hours,
Give me a purpose
For each coming hour.

To see your light shining bright,
Deliver me
From this fight,
Please give me a purpose for today.

Some days hope seems
A long way off,
Give me your strength to see
Your mountain top.

Your glory abides
In great magnitude,
Give me a purpose for today
To help me through.

WHEN WORDS ARE LOST IN FATHOMS DEEP

Teardrops rise up inside
When emotions run high,
Feelings emerge from weakened nerves
Shattered by some news I heard.

The passage to the heart so fine
When words or thoughts run dry,
This part of us that makes us weep
When words are lost in fathoms deep.

Circumstances cause the pain
We just can't express,
That's when words are lost in fathoms deep,
Sometimes it's for the best.

Time is a great healer
Give it all to the Saviour,
Sometimes words must silent be
For healing to come to me.

YOUR HOLY PLAN

Help me Lord to believe in myself
On the days that don't seem to shine,
Clouds hover overhead
That affect this heart of mine.

Staying in my comfort zone,
It's so easy to do,
But life carries no thrill to seek
If I don't have a distant view.

Doubt stands up to rule my head
To say "you never will",
Give me your strength Lord
So your plan will be fulfilled.

Charge me with your Spirit divine
So I can take your precious hand,
Help me to do all things
In your Holy plan.

KEEP ME COVERED

Keep me covered Lord
Under your wings,
Protect me, shield me
From the hurt that living brings.

Keep me covered Lord
With your skies of blue,
Take this hurt away
To the sunshine in you.

Keep me covered Lord
With your divine, endless love,
Thank you for your promise
Of your eternal home above.

EMOTION

Our morality gets in the way,
We let emotion have its say,
Temptation is hard to beat,
We crumble in our fragility.

Pride it seems to rule our lives,
Scorn stands up to cross the line,
Patience doesn't stand a chance,
Jealousy does a merry dance.

When we ask the Lord to assist,
Failure doesn't even exist,
Trust all things will come right,
He will move in our lives.

Try not to focus on negative thoughts
That pile up one after the other,
Claim the truth of God's love,
His peace you will discover.

Make His will your goal
In all you do every day,
His divine love will intercede,
Talk to the Father, you will succeed.

CLAIM HIS RIGHTEOUSNESS

Claim His righteousness
And His reign of peace,
Make it earnest prayer
At His Holy seat.

Claim His righteousness
To shield your heart,
To give you wealth in truth
And the need to do your part.

We need His glorious creation
To be kept in perfect working order,
To restore the wealth He gave us
At home and across our borders.

Claim His righteousness,
For honesty and hope,
To protect this mighty world
For future vision scope.

WINTER CHILLS

Don't let winter steal your heart
It's easy so to do,
Tell the Master when you're down,
He sure will carry you through.

Trust Him as your confidante,
He wants to know your all,
He'll take those winter chills away
And melt the snow that falls.

Life will have its rainy days
But don't forget He's there,
He wants to warm your heart and soul,
Your cares and hurts He'll bear.

His warmth will clear away the fog
So you will clearly see
His wondrous face before your eyes,
He's all you'll ever need.

PART THREE

"I will be your father,
and you shall be my
sons and daughters,
says the Lord Almighty."

2 Corinthians 6 : 18

REST…
UNDER HIS WINGS…

"…have peace by being united to me…"

John 16 : 33

SONS AND DAUGHTERS OF THE KING

No matter what the future holds
We are sons and daughters of the King,
Prayer and praises to His name
We must surely bring.

Don't think about tomorrow,
His plan for you He'll bring,
In His love you are safe,
Sons and daughters of the King.

Life will bring its trials,
Sure enough that is true,
But with Him by your side
There's nothing you can't do.

As sons and daughters of the King,
His name you must uphold,
To live a righteous life each day,
In His Word it is told.

So raise your hand in worship
When in praise you sing
To the Saviour of the world,
Sons and daughters of the King.

HE CAN'T WAIT TO MEET YOU

The Lord can't wait to meet you,
His beloved you are,
He loves you so much
He wants you just as you are!

He can't wait to meet you
After your journey ends,
You'll have so much to share
And you'll see the rainbow's end.

He can't wait to meet you,
You are always in His sight,
Every challenge He meets with you
And your every tear He wipes.

He mends your broken heart
Then when you think He doesn't care,
He empowers His angels
To protect you everywhere.

He can't wait to meet you
For you to receive a golden crown,
And the rewards He has waiting
Because your sin cannot be found.

HIS BELOVED

We are His beloved,
He loves us endlessly,
He wants us all to live
In His perfect harmony.

We are His beloved,
In His image we are,
A plan for each of us,
And a place amongst the stars.

We are His beloved
By our side He'll always be,
He'll never stop loving us,
In all Eternity.

We are His beloved,
He craves for us so,
To simply say "I love you"
Then His Spirit we will own.

SEA OF WORDS

Lay your peace on me Lord
When I read your Holy Word
Worries cease for a while
When I'm lost in your sea of words.

Answers are always found
When your heart needs binding up,
Open His book to any page
You will find His words of love.

Through centuries of time there's always been
Hearts that struggle and fear,
You'll find His words of comfort
Just turn the pages there.

On the days that are the hardest
Leave The Bible open wide,
So that when you walk past it,
His words you will find.

Sea of words printed on the page
That speak so loud to you,
You'll feel His hands around your heart
And His love to help you through.

WE ALL NEED THE SAVIOUR'S LOVE

We all need the Saviour's love,
That brings healing and stability
To the open heart
That bruises easily.

You owe it to yourself
To care for emotions inside,
Ask for His peace and calm
In you to abide.

Look to the Saviour
When worries come along,
To keep you balanced
He will make you strong.

He cares for you so much
No matter who you are,
We all need the Saviour's love
As we journey near and far.

SERVE OF LOVE

Open His Good Book
For a serve of love,
You will see inside His heart,
You will feel His wondrous love.

When the world makes you tired
And you need to step away,
Open His holy pages,
Refresh your thoughts today.

Lift your sight to His heavenly loft,
Fly free for a little while,
His holy balm will soothe you
If you seek His holy smile.

Come to the Saviour for a serve of love,
He wants to know what's on your mind,
His pierced hands are waiting
To mend your heart inside.

LIFE'S JOURNEY...
HE KNOWS EACH DAY...

"Peace is what I leave with you;
it is my own peace that I give you..."

John 14 : 27

MARCH IN STEP

Thank you Dear One
For always being there,
When I want to talk
You always care.

When I feel thankful,
It's wonderful to say,
I hope it warms your heart
In some small way.

Any care at any time
I can give to you,
Your ear is always listening
Help me see your point of view.

Your plan may be different
To the one I had in mind
But help me to be patient
While I march in step in time.

REACH FOR THE SAVIOUR

My pillow is His shoulder
When cares fill my head,
I struggle to sleep
As I lay in my bed.

He keeps me close
As His arms come near,
His shelter I reach for
Away from my fears.

Think thoughts of His greatness,
There's nothing He can't do,
Think of the Saviour
He will take the fear in you.

He will restore your peace
And calm in your life,
Reach for the Saviour
He will hold you tight.

PEACE TIME

Peace time, is when we meet alone,
I call you to my side,
I find the words I want to say
And confess what lies inside.

To talk to you, one to one
I feel your focus on me,
I whisper my prayers to you,
You are with me instantly.

Please comfort me and tell me
Things will be alright,
I ask for your strength
To guide me through the night.

Peace time is quiet time,
I feel your Spirit near,
Thank you Lord for all you do,
Take my inner fears.

QUESTIONS AND ANSWERS

Human nature,
So complex and vast,
Only God has the answers
To questions you may ask.

Stories of life
Fill the pages of His Word,
You can be sure
No stone is left unturned.

So turn the pages of His Word
For questions in your mind,
Anytime take a moment,
The answer you will find.

NEVER GIVE UP ON HOPE

Life has its moments
Of ups and downs,
Tears and joy
Laughter and frowns.

But we can choose happiness over sadness,
To look for the positives of life,
We can wrap ourselves in His gladness,
To walk in His light.

Don't let shadows cast
A veil over you,
Be strong in the love of Christ,
He will never abandon you.

Never give up on hope
That sunshine will break through,
Christ our shining light,
He always loves you.

MY FAINTING HEART

I feel like I'm in a desolate place,
My heart it doesn't sing,
Happiness seems to pass me by,
Emotion lies dead within.

I feel no call to "soldier on"
I've lost my way it seems,
Why am I in "no-man's-land"?
From this rut I have to flee.

Give me strength to rise above
This pit of misery,
Take me to a higher place
Bring your wings to rescue me.

Open my eyes to see your light
And your radiant beams to reach
My inner soul and fainting heart,
Your Throne I have to seek.

PART FOUR

"When I am lifted up from the earth,
I will draw everyone to me."

John 12 : 32

FORGIVENESS…
FOR ALL…

"I am telling you the truth: he who believes has eternal life."

John 6 : 47

AS IT IS WRITTEN

As prophesied in His Word,
A Messiah would come,
Born in a manger
He would grow to be God's Son.

A precious life like no other,
A heart full of love,
He was tempted in everyway
But to sin did not succumb.

His miracles were a witness
That He was the Son of God,
The wind and sea obeyed Him,
But believe; the crowd would not.

They still sent Him to the Cross,
No words He did reply,
When tried for His innocence,
They shouted "crucify"!

And so, as it is written,
A Messiah did come,
Innocent yet crucified,
God's own precious Son.

A BRAND NEW LOVE

A brand new love is waiting
To touch a lonely heart,
It comes from Eternity
With grace, peace and calm.

This brand new love so mighty,
Comes with a Holy Crown,
Held in pierced hands
That together, once were bound.

This brand new love
Is just a breath away,
Whisper "Saviour come,
Change me now today."

With your brand new love
You will never be alone,
Forever you are His
When you bow before His Throne.

THE COMMUNION CUP

Surround yourself with peace,
Be touched by joy divine,
Behold His glorious presence,
The Lord, the one true vine.

Feel deep His Spirit within
That brings His holy love,
Let it nurture and bless you,
You will know His peace from above.

When you share His Communion Cup
It symbolizes His blood shed for you,
When we break the bread in His name,
Represents His body given too.

This drove Him to Calvary,
He bore your sins to set you free,
We take the Cup in remembrance
For what He did for you and me.

ETERNAL LIFE…
WAS BORN…

"…Then Jesus came and stood among them. "Peace be with you," He said. After saying this, he showed them his hands and his side."… "Then he breathed on them and said, "Receive the Holy Spirit."

John 20 : 19, 20, 22

HE LIVES TODAY

There's gladness in my heart
Because He lives today,
Gladness in my heart,
He is the only way.

He took the Cross at Calvary,
It was His Father's will,
In agony He looked beyond
To a Throne above the hill.

He was obedient to the end
Of His ministry on earth,
So we could have eternal life
That's why He came to serve.

His heavenly Father raised Him,
A victor o'er the grave,
Death no longer claimed Him,
He rose; He lives today!

THE WONDER OF HIS LOVE

The chosen Son of God
Came to earth for victory,
He bought our redemption
With His life at Calvary.

His precious blood was shed
For all mankind,
Blameless He stood;
No sin in Him to find.

His eyes were set on Heaven
But the Cross was on His path,
"Father not my will but yours"
The Saviour asked.

The wonder of His love
Is His Spirit He left behind
As He made His way to Heaven
For His family to find.

JESUS…
CHRISTMAS JOY…

"…when they saw the child with his mother Mary, they knelt down and worshiped him. They brought out their gifts of gold, frankincense and myrrh, and presented them to him."

Matthew 2 : 11

CHRISTMAS EVE SUPPERS

There's something about Christmas,
People decorate their house,
They seem kinder to each other,
That's so good I want to shout!

Christmas Eve so special,
Suppers are the best,
Families get together,
The time I love the best.

My Aunties and Uncles would join the family,
Such a special time,
We'd all bring a plate to share
And a gift for under the tree.

It may have been a hundred degrees outside
And the stars were shining bright,
We were all together
It's Christmas Eve tonight!

Thank you Lord for family and the gift of You.

FRANKINCENSE, MYRRH AND GOLD

Frankincense, Myrrh and Gold
Are the gifts for the Lord
Bought to Him by the Magi,
They came to worship and adore.

On the first Holy night
They were led by the Eastern Star,
Gifts so significant,
Lovingly carried from afar.

Scripture prophesied
A Messiah would come,
In a lowly manger He lay,
God's precious Son.

Frankincense marks His birth,
Myrrh for a sacrifice to come,
Gold reserved for Kings,
The gifts for the Holy One.

These gifts revered for the Saviour
Will be known for all time,
Holy down through the ages,
Frankincense, Myrrh and Gold; divine.

JOY ON CHRISTMAS MORNING

I woke Christmas morning
As sun was stretching high,
Anticipation in the air,
Christmas was nigh.

There is joy in the air
As we wake on Christmas Day,
When two thousand years ago
It was Jesus' birthday.

His angels sang in unity
To the shepherds in the fields,
Of the Lord's arrival
In a stable over the hills.

The star in the East
Shone like a diamond in the sky,
Above the stable beams
Glory from on high.

The Messiah's arrival
In the stable here below,
He came to save the world
Because He loves us so.

I KNEW HIM FROM A CHILD

I knew Him from a child
From my Sunday School days,
Memories shine bright
That bought His love my way.

Bible stories awoke
His story to me,
How Bethlehem bought the Babe
Whose sight was on Calvary.

He came to teach the world
Of His heavenly love,
He is the Holy Son Himself,
Sent from God above.

So I knew Him as a child,
His path I found so young,
One day He will return
To take us all beyond the Sun.

ALSO BY CLAIRE GROSE

This is Claire's first book of inspirational poems to help others through the challenges of life.
They are inspired by God's love which is for everyone.

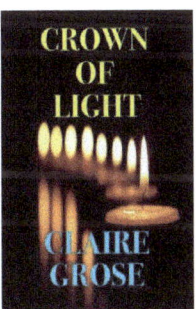

This is Claire's second book of poems, inspired by the glorious radiance of Christ. It covers His beauty around us in Mother Earth, the sheer joy of knowing His love, the inspirational hope and strength available to us if we ask Him, and His salvation and redemption to all who will believe in Him.

ABOUT THE AUTHOR

Claire worked as a Government Public Servant in the Lands Department, Adelaide, South Australia until she married and became a mother of two boys.

She later returned to the work force during which time she gained a "Living Hope" Phone Counselling certificate which influenced her need to help others.

Through this and personal experience she found herself inspired by God's love to put pen to paper.

PHOTO CREDITS

Cover photo: Lugano, Switzerland – Michael and Andrea
Page 2: Waterfall Gully, S.A. – Claire Grose
Page 12: Lavender, Stansbury, S.A. – Claire Grose
Page 24: Gum Trees, Kallangur, Qld – Chris and Justine Turner
Page 31: Agapanthus, Hewett, S.A. – Lindsay Grose
Page 39: Daisies, Paralowie, S.A. – June and Hugh Kennedy
Page 48: Flowering Gums, Hewett, S.A. – Lindsay Grose
Page 56: Grevilleas, Witta, Qld. – Carol and Den Turner
Page 71: Waterfall Gully, S.A. – Claire Grose
Page 79: Bird Bath, Blair Athol, S.A. – Karen and Jeff Cluse
Page 88: Salisbury Uniting Church Cross, Salisbury, S.A.
Page 93: Glass Window: Stansbury, S.A. – Jane and Scott Helmore
Page 97: Poinsettias, Witta, Qld. – Carol and Den Turner